Full STEAM Ahead!
Arts in Action

Making Music

Robin Johnson

CRABTREE
PUBLISHING COMPANY
WWW.CRABTREEBOOKS.COM

Title-Specific Learning Objectives:
Readers will:
- Explain how sounds are made by vibrations.
- Describe the characteristics of the four families of instruments.
- Identify a variety of instruments and explain how they relate to each other.

High-frequency words (grade one)	Academic vocabulary
all, are, by, can, have, into, make, of, that, with	device, family, instruments, music, pitch, vibrate

Before, During, and After Reading Prompts:

Activate Prior Knowledge and Make Predictions:
Have a number of simple instruments on display as children come into the room. These could include a drum, a tambourine, a xylophone, a flute, a small horn, and a stringed instrument. Next, ask children which one word describes all of these things. The word is "instruments." Ask how many of them have instruments at home, or know how to play one.

Next, have children read pages 6 and 7 of the book. Ask what they think the rest of the book will be about.

During Reading:
After reading pages 14 and 15, ask children what all of the instruments on the pages have in common. They should see that they all have a long piece with holes, and need the musician to blow air into them. Explain that instruments in each family share certain things.

After Reading:
Have children draw four columns on a piece of paper. At the top of each column, they should write the name of an instrument family. Have them work in groups to list as many instruments as they can in each column without looking in the book. Encourage them to also add instruments they know about that were not in the book. Make a master chart on the board, rotating through the groups as you add instruments.

Author: Robin Johnson
Series Development: Reagan Miller
Editors: Bonnie Dobkin, Janine Deschenes
Proofreader: Melissa Boyce
STEAM Notes for Educators: Bonnie Dobkin
Guided Reading Leveling: Publishing Solutions Group
Cover, Interior Design, and Prepress: Samara Parent
Photo research: Robin Johnson and Samara Parent

Production coordinator: Katherine Berti

Photographs:
Alamy: Ted Foxx: p. 21 (b)
iStock: FatCamer: p. 5 (t); izusek: p. 7 (b)
Shutterstock: Melting Spot: cover; Ghina photography: p. 9 (tl); T photography: p. 10; akiyoko: p. 11 (b); Sergey Dobrydnev: p. 13 (t); Luisa Fumi: p. 15 (b); Vera NewSib: p. 19 (t); Louise Wateridge: p. 20

All other photographs by Shutterstock

Library and Archives Canada Cataloguing in Publication

Title: Making music / Robin Johnson.
Names: Johnson, Robin (Robin R.), author.
Description: Series statement: Full STEAM ahead! | Includes index.
Identifiers: Canadiana (print) 20200165801 |
 Canadiana (ebook) 2020016581X |
 ISBN 9780778771913 (hardcover) |
 ISBN 9780778772699 (softcover) |
 ISBN 9781427124623 (HTML)
Subjects: LCSH: Musical instruments—Juvenile literature.
Classification: LCC ML460 .J68 2020 | DDC j784.192/2—dc23

Library of Congress Cataloging-in-Publication Data

Names: Johnson, Robin (Robin R.) author.
Title: Making music / Robin Johnson.
Description: New York : Crabtree Publishing Company, 2020. |
 Series: Full STEAM ahead! | Includes index.
Identifiers: LCCN 2019058740 (print) | LCCN 2019058741 (ebook) |
 ISBN 9780778771913 (hardcover) |
 ISBN 9780778772699 (paperback) | ISBN 9781427124623 (ebook)
Subjects: LCSH: Musical instruments--Juvenile literature.
Classification: LCC ML460 .J68 2020 (print) | LCC ML460 (ebook) |
 DDC 784.192/2--dc23
LC record available at https://lccn.loc.gov/2019058740
LC ebook record available at https://lccn.loc.gov/2019058741

Printed in the U.S.A./032020/CG20200127

Table of Contents

Making Music 4

Musical Instruments 6

Family Groups 8

Strings 10

Woodwinds 12

Brass 14

Percussion 16

The Right Pitch 18

Playing Together 20

Words to Know 22

Index and About the Author 23

Crabtree Plus Digital Code 23

STEAM Notes for Educators 24

Crabtree Publishing Company
www.crabtreebooks.com　　1-800-387-7650

Copyright © 2020 CRABTREE PUBLISHING COMPANY. All rights reserved. No part of this publication may be reproduced, stored in a retrieval system or be transmitted in any form or by any means, electronic, mechanical, photocopying, recording, or otherwise, without the prior written permission of Crabtree Publishing Company. In Canada: We acknowledge the financial support of the Government of Canada through the Canada Book Fund for our publishing activities.

Published in Canada
Crabtree Publishing
616 Welland Ave.
St. Catharines, Ontario
L2M 5V6

Published in the United States
Crabtree Publishing
PMB 59051
350 Fifth Avenue, 59th Floor
New York, New York 10118

Published in the United Kingdom
Crabtree Publishing
Maritime House
Basin Road North, Hove
BN41 1WR

Published in Australia
Crabtree Publishing
Unit 3 – 5 Currumbin Court
Capalaba
QLD 4157

Making Music

There are so many ways to make music! You can sing and clap your hands. You can play a guitar. You can blow a horn or bang a drum. How do you like to make music?

These girls are having fun making music. One girl blows a trumpet. The other girl hits a tambourine.

It is fun to make music with other people.

This boy is playing a violin to make music.

5

Musical Instruments

Some people use instruments to make music. Instruments are objects that make sounds. There are many different instruments played around the world. They all make something **vibrate** to create sounds.

The strings on these instruments vibrate when they are played.

This musician in Peru is playing the pipes. Blowing in them makes air vibrate.

Musicians hit the material stretched across a drum to make it vibrate.

Family Groups

Musical instruments are put into groups called families. The instruments in each family are played in a similar way.

These instruments are all hit to make sounds. They are in the percussion family.

A trumpet uses air to make sounds. It belongs to the brass family.

Instruments in the string family all have strings that are used to make music.

These instruments are in the woodwind family. Musicians blow into them to make sounds.

Strings

Instruments in this family all have strings. The strings are **strummed**, **plucked**, or played with a **bow**. Some string instruments are the guitar, violin, cello, and harp.

These musicians in Greece are playing string instruments. One musician uses a bow. The other strums the strings with his fingers.

Guitars have strings that are plucked or strummed. Some guitars can be plugged into **devices** that make their sounds louder.

The koto is a string instrument played in Japan. It has strings that are plucked.

Woodwinds

Instruments in this family are played by blowing air into an opening or **mouthpiece**. Some woodwind instruments are the flute, saxophone, oboe, and clarinet.

Some woodwind mouthpieces use a thin piece of wood called a reed. The reed vibrates when people blow air across it.

Most woodwinds have metal parts called keys. Musicians press the keys to cover the holes and change the sound.

clarinet

This flute is a woodwind instrument. Woodwinds can be made out of wood, metal, clay, and other materials.

This long, thick bassoon makes a deep sound.

13

Brass

Another family is called brass instruments. Musicians play these instruments by blowing air into a mouthpiece while vibrating their lips. Trumpets, trombones, French horns, and tubas are some brass instruments.

Most brass instruments are made of a shiny yellow metal called brass.

French horn

Many brass instruments, such as the French horn, have keys.

These musicians are playing tubas and trombones.

tuba

trombone

15

Percussion

Percussion instruments like drums make up a large family. These instruments make sounds when they are hit, rubbed, or shaken. The xylophone, triangle, tambourine, and bell are also percussion instruments.

This musician is playing a xylophone called a pong lang. It is a percussion instrument from Thailand.

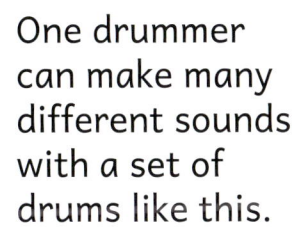

One drummer can make many different sounds with a set of drums like this.

A triangle is a percussion instrument that is hit with a metal stick.

Maracas are percussion instruments from Mexico. They are shaken to make sound.

17

The Right Pitch

Musical instruments have different pitches. Pitch describes how high or low a sound is.

String instruments with thick strings, such as cellos, make low-pitched sounds.

String instruments with thin strings, such as violins, make high-pitched sounds.

Keys on brass instruments can change the pitch. Trombones have sliding tubes that change the sound. Musicians also change pitch by changing how they blow into the mouthpiece.

Musicians change the pitch of woodwind instruments by covering holes with their fingers or pressing keys.

chimes

Percussion instruments with different sizes and shapes make different sounds. Some percussion instruments have pieces with different pitches. The shorter pieces on this set of chimes have higher pitches than the longer ones.

19

Playing Together

Musicians often play together to make different kinds of music. Some play just for fun. Some play music for others to enjoy.

Musicians make beautiful music when they play different kinds of instruments together. This marching band has musicians who play percussion and brass instruments.

These friends work together to learn how to play their favorite rock song.

An orchestra is a group of musicians who play different kinds of instruments. They **perform** for an audience. What kinds of instruments are used by this orchestra?

21

Words to Know

bow [bow] noun A wooden stick that has horsehair stretched across it. It is used to play string instruments.

device [dih-VAHYS] noun A machine or piece of equipment that does a certain job

mouthpiece [MOUTH-pees] noun The piece of an instrument onto which a musician puts his or her mouth

perform [per-FAWRM] verb To put on a show for people to watch

plucked [pluhk-ed] verb Pulled strings to make sounds

strummed [struhm-ed] verb Brushed strings to make sounds

vibrate [VAHY-breyt] verb To move quickly back and forth

A noun is a person, place, or thing.
A verb is an action word that tells you what someone or something does.
An adjective is a word that tells you what something is like.

Index

brass instruments 4, 9, 14–15, 19, 20
keys 12, 15, 19
materials 7, 12–14, 17
mouthpiece 12, 14, 19
percussion instruments 4, 7, 8, 16–17, 19, 20
string instruments 5, 6, 9–11, 18, 21
vibrate 6–7, 12, 14
woodwind instruments 7, 9, 12–13, 19

About the Author

Robin Johnson is a freelance author and editor who has written more than 80 children's books. When she isn't working, Robin builds castles in the sky with her engineer husband and their two best creations—sons Jeremy and Drew.

To explore and learn more, enter the code at the Crabtree Plus website below.

www.crabtreeplus.com/fullsteamahead

Your code is:
fsa20

STEAM Notes for Educators

Full STEAM Ahead is a literacy series that helps readers build vocabulary, fluency, and comprehension while learning about big ideas in STEAM subjects. *Making Music* introduces readers to connections within a text as they identify characteristics common to all the instruments in a particular family. The STEAM activity below helps readers extend the ideas in the book to build their understanding of technology and the arts.

Shoe-Box Guitar

Children will be able to:
- Explain how vibrations create sound.
- Follow directions for building a simple instrument.
- Demonstrate their understanding of pitch.

Materials
- Shoe-Box Guitar Direction Sheet
- Materials to create guitar (one per child): shoe box, rubber bands of different lengths and thicknesses (must fit around the length of the shoe box), safety scissors, pencils, and paper-towel tube
- Supplies for decorating

Guiding Prompts
After reading *Making Music*, ask children:
- How are musical sounds made?
- What are four different families of instruments?

Activity Prompts
Have children read pages 10 and 11. Ask:
- What are string instruments?

Then, turn to pages 18 and 19. Ask:
- What is pitch?
- How are different pitches created on string instruments?

Tell children that they will be able to experiment with pitch by making their own shoe-box guitar. Ask if any children play guitar or know someone who does. Ask them to describe the instrument, then invite volunteers to demonstrate how a guitar is played.

Distribute the Shoe-Box Guitar Direction Sheet and supplies to each student. Make sure each child has many more rubber bands than he or she will need, in a variety of sizes and thicknesses.

Remind children that before they begin their project, they should read all of the directions to see if they understand them. Allow them time to do so and ask questions. Then have them build their guitars. Consider having a shoe-box guitar concert when they are done!

Extensions
- Make sure students understand the science behind their guitars by asking them: Which rubber band makes the highest sound? Which makes the lowest? Why? How would your guitar sound if you cut a hole in the box?

> To view and download the worksheet, visit **www.crabtreebooks.com/resources/printables** or **www.crabtreeplus.com/fullsteamahead** and enter the code **fsa20**.